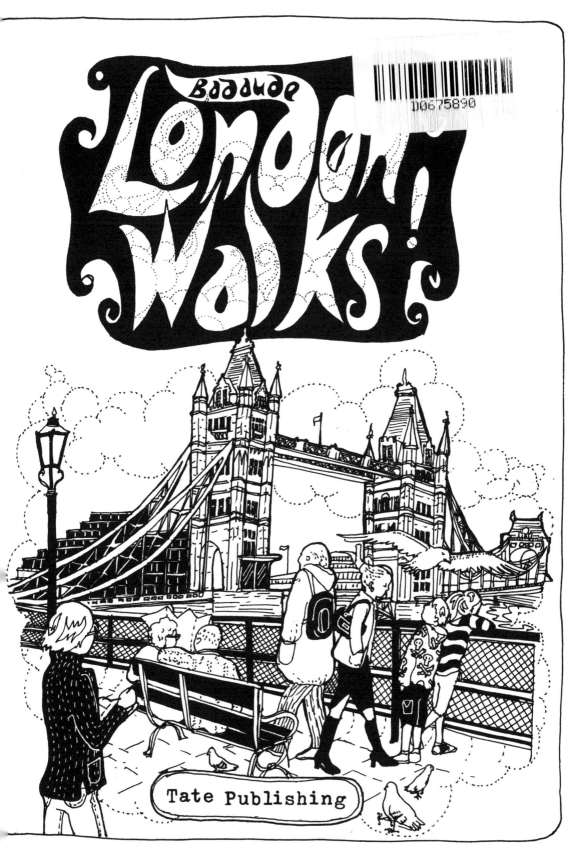

In this book, you will find 22 walks, 3 bus rides & 1 boat trip. Walks are generally 1-2 miles long and can be combined to create longer journeys. My maps contain no recommended routes: start and end your journey at any point taking the route that pleases you best.

What's up here?
Always look beyond the first storey
Is everyone a local or a visitor?
Are they watching you?
or someone else?
Look at the street furniture
What is being sold
and at what price?
and the local decor
Which bits of the past are crumbling?
This building condemned KEEP O
GOLF SALE TODAY
Can you get in here?
FREE PAPER
FREE PAPER
and which are preserved?
or slow?
Kelly Vintage
If you walk in cities, you will see so muc !
Window-shop in Bond Street, Sloane Street, Oxford Street... Try something on. Looking is always free!
Create your own London tour on city buses. (Sit at the top front seat for a rollercoaster ride)
And finally cities change: if the museums, the markets, the cafés in this book change or disappear, remember that London reinvents itself and this book is only the starting point for you to invent your own guide to London

walk 1 OXFORD CIRCUS DESIRES

Where better to start than at the target-centre of the tube map and of our consumer desires?

Look up past Oxford Street's first-storey plate-glass-caged fashion mannequins to wider, wilder desires...

John Lewis department store features a "winged figure" (1962) sculpted by Barbara Hepworth

Two angels (but what's in fashion for this season's angels: draping or angles?)

Eric Gill's 1932 Portland Place relief panels for the BBC depicting Prospero and Ariel were attacked for provoking DESIRE

Portland Place = Regent Street

The Queen of Time rides the ship of commerce above the the revolving door of Selfridges department store. How long do I have to shop?

Oxford Circus

Oxford Street

buyers (western)

producers (eastern)

To Marble Arch

LESS LUST BY LESS PROTEIN: MEAT FISH BIRD: EGG CHEESE: PEAS BEANS NUTS. AND SITTING

Regent Street

The 1914 Regent Street neoclassical facade of department store, **Liberty** couldn't be more at odds with its cosy mock-Tudor more famous building behind. **Britannia** presides over a shopping chain: the East providing and the West consuming. The two figures peeping over the parapet above the elephant are stone too.

From 1968 to 1993, Stanley Green campaigned against long-forgotten sins, aiming to reduce desire on this most lustful of streets

remember keep looking up wherever you are...

Fitzrovia Facades

Was the area beloved of the 20th century's <u>writers</u> artists and ad-men ever more than a fiction?

> George Bernard Shaw lived here...

Plane trees cause pollution of their own: their leave can aggravate asthma & are slow to decompose

If Fitzrovia

lacks Oxford Street's plate-glass facades and retains a neighbourhood atmosphere with small independent pubs, cafés and shops, remember it is also where the <u>dream factories</u> of literature, broadcasting, advertising & fashion have their headquarters...

Fitzroy Square is empty. No cars, no people. It could be 1930.

The London Plane tree is perfectly adapted to life in the city, being <del>London</del> grey and shedding its pollution-absorbing outer bark.

Walk 2: Avoiding Oxford Street

The Wallace Collection

Manchester Square

The Wigmore Hall

Edgware Road

Baker Street

Sometimes the best way to see Oxford Street's monster department stores is from behind: delivery entrances on calm squares of redbrick mansions, so different from their hectic (portland) stony faced Oxford Street entrances.

BBC Building (Eric Gill frescoes)

Wigmore Street   Cavendish Pl.

Seymour St.

Marble Arch   M&S   Selfridges   Bond Street   Debenhams House of Fraser John Lewis   Oxfo

Marylebone, the area <u>West</u> of Oxford Circus is often confused with

Confusingly, although Virginia Woolf was a member of what came to be called the Blooms-bury Group, Fitzroy Square is not in Blooms-bury which lies East of Tottenham Court Road

.. as did Virginia Woolf (not at the same time)

The building now houses a firm of accountants.

The name Fitzrovia ~ after the

FitzroyTavern

is said to have been coined by "Poetry London" editor, Tambi (Meary James Thurairajah Tambimuttu) during the 1930s

Noho?

Nowhere?

In 2008 developers tried to rebrand the site of the former Middlesex Hospital, "Noho Square", extending the name to the surrounding area "North of Soho". After community protests the name was with-drawn but for how long can Fitzrovia hold on to its interwar charm?

Euston Road

Warren Street

Fitzroy Square

Pollock's Toy Museum

Fitzroy street

The Post Office (now BT) Tower (Maple street)

Scala street
Goodge Street

street

Fitzrovia Residents

have included: Augustus John Quentin Crisp, Dylan Thomas, Aleister Crowley, Nina Hamnett, George Orwell, Charles Laughton, Elsa Lanchester, Thomas Paine, Edmund Burke, Paul Verlaine, Arthur Rimbaud, Patrick Kavanagh.

Old Middlesex Hospital

Mortimer street

Goodge

The Wheat Sheaf

pub to which post-war Fitzrovians 'decamped' after the Fitzroy became "too popular"

Charlotte st.

Percy street

Many small fry end up here not seeming to want to reach busy Tottenham Court Road

Tottenham Court Road

Rathbone Pl.

red brick mansions
Portland stone

CharlotteStreet (cafés, Soho bars, restaurants...)

Fitzrovia which lies to the North and East of the tube station

Lost Illusions

Tottenham Court Road

publishing · advertising

Charing Cross Road

Soho Square (office workers eating lunch)

Hazlitt's Hotel (once the house where the writer lived & died).

Soho Square where homeless writer Thomas de Quincey, was helped by prostitute, Anne. He tried to trace her in later life but found she had disappeared.

Fifth street

To Foyles Bookshop

Bar Italia the orig-inal 1950s cafe-bar.

Greek Street

St Martin's School of Art's Art Deco Facade

To the site of The Magic Shop on Tottenham Court Road where an edition of John Cleland's naughty 1748 novel, Fanny Hill, appeared in 1963 ~ then magic-ally disappeared after a police raid

First impressions are often the truest as we find (to our cost) not infrequently when we have been wheedled out of them

William Hazlitt

Oscar Wilde

Old Compton Street

moor st.

The French House

Maison Bertaux

Kettners where Oscar Wilde met the man who would betray him in court, and where he was arrested before being taken to the nearby Magistrate's Court in Great Marlborough St.

My first impressions of people are invari- ably right *

+ William Hazlitt ~ On the knowledge of character

* The Importance of Being Earnest

Is it a Trick?

SOHO on a wet afternoon

CINO ESPRESSO

Illusion

Outdoor tables outside the French and Italian cafés despite the British Weather (we're a European country, right?) By 1720, Huguenot refugees had made Soho a French-speaking enclave.

Light?
The rain makes everything as shiny as the latex that still fills the windows between the coffee bars and the design studios. It gathers in slick puddles. Meaning slips. Is everything as it seems on the wet pavement?
On the opposite side of Old Compton Street are two beautiful young men, one of them obviously drunk, the other worried, tugging his friend's arm. They wait on the corner, the drunk's arm raised as though hailing a taxi. Eventually a car stops. They get in. I drink m
after 20 minutes, the two boys are back. And was that long enough to turn a trick?
Wha I see?
pink champagne

Walk 4 Down **Utopia Row**

Tottenham Ct. Rd.

Charing Cross Rd.

From the British Museum's reading room where (amongst others) Marx, Lenin, Wells, Orwell, Woolf & Shaw wrote Utopias and Dystopias, along _Theobald's Road_ where an unusual number of idealistic _societies_ have been hatched

New Oxford Street   Bloomsbury Way

DUCK into Tottenham Court Road tube station to see mosaic murals by **Eduardo Paolozzi**

St Giles High Street

The **Swedenborg** 20 **Society** whose founder saw a vision of Christ in a London Pub.

High Holborn

Southampton Row

the **central School of Art** founded in 1896, influenced by the ideas of utopian Socialists John Ruskin & William Morris's

Installation

caps

scarves sweets

gloves

gloves hats

chocolate

cigarettes

chilled drinks

umbrellas, maps, toys, slippers.

YVE
KLE
vs
MBC
KL

The **Kiosk** on Theobald's Road sells _city_ essentials - anything and everything - from a large green metal _box_ that folds away each evening

The kiosk does not appear to sell newspapers

Coram's Fields

The National Sunday League met at 8 Theobald's Road to campaign for a **weekly Utopia**[8]

In 1739 Thomas Coram returned from the American colonies to open a <u>foundling</u> hospital for the abandoned children that he was <u>shocked</u> to discover everywhere in London (the site is now a park and playground)

Lamb's Conduit Street

John Street

Gray's Inn Road

Theobald's Road

The Garden of LOVE

80 Sadlers Wells

Rosebery Avenue

The <u>Griffin</u> "Gentleman's Club" an earthly Paradise - of a kind...

Clerkenwell Road

The Ethical Society met here at the <u>Conway Hall</u> as did the <u>Order of the Golden Dawn</u>.

Gray's Inn Field

In 1711 the gardener was "ordered to admit "no ordinary men" & no " women or children"+ 'Thou shalt not' writ over the door *

125 89

>> International magic

London's last dedicated high street magic shop.

Hatton Garden for wedding rings

Bleeding Heart Yard ↓

Saffron Hill

+ The pension book of Gray's Inn, 1711   * William Blake ~ the Garden of Love

---

Central Saint Martin's college of Art

occupied 2011 this site for the last century before a move to a purpose-built development in King's cross, designed to house the new art school.

Hidden London

The old Kingsway Tram Tunnel, closed in 1957 once took single-decker trams under London to Waterloo. Opened in 1906 it has remained un-used though in 2009 it was home to an installation by the artist Conrad Shawcross

The Italianate portico of Sicilian Avenue

A little Italy of outdoor cafés selling reassuringly British cling-film wrapped sandwiches

PACE!

The Boat 'race crews pull for the West like the dreams of Londoners. Hammersmith is a *Floating World* suspended between the river and the flyover. Are we in the city or the country? Should we stop here or just keep on going?

Ralph Erskine's **Ar.** office building in Talgarth Road sails West and is named (accidentally?) after the boat in which William Morris went West to die at Kelmscott in 1896

Hoodies, rugby shirts, cargo pants: I have never seen so many **Leisure** clothes

still floats Thames de reconstruct 1 foiled bom

Br

me highway.

The Ark →

Walk 5: The Floating World

Hammersmith Flyover

Furnival Gardens

Blue nor Publ ou

13

The Thames

Hammersmith Bridge Rd

you've already passed **The World's End** (The World's End Chelsea that is) →

The *Ukiyo-e* or Floating World of Japanese art portrays a land of "Cockaigne" or infinite leisure and sensual pleasure. The word "Cockney" ~ or **pampered** city-dweller ~ possibly comes from the same root.

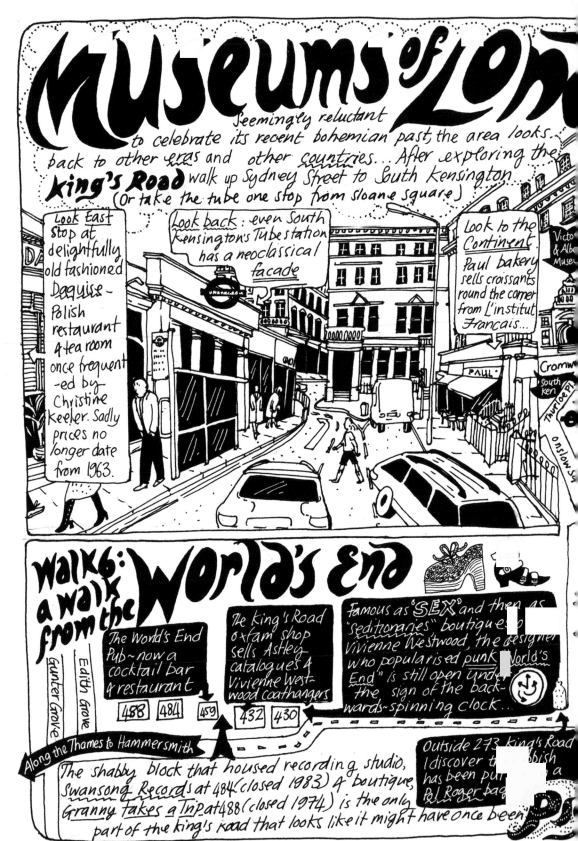

The Cast Court at the Victoria & Albert Museum

Better than the real thing. Visit the museum's surprising collection of casts of major artworks collected by Henry Cole and John Charles Robinson during the 19th century. Many are now in better condition than the originals.

"Pillar" would not fit in the new gallery so is displayed cut into two halves.

Look out for the pickpocket on the lower half of Trajan's column...

The 'V&A' was set up in 1851 as a teaching collection. Art students drew the casts, learning anatomy and technique, without having to encounter real nudes.

Too much like the real thing? The copy of Michelangelo's David was deemed too explicitly nude for Queen Victoria's eyes and a plaster fig leaf (now exhibited behind the statue) was kept in case of royal visits.

It's difficult to imagine that The King's Road was ever a centre of hippy then punk rebellion in the 1960s and 70s

Once the Chelsea Drugstore, namechecked by the Rolling Stones, from which a squad of girls in purple catsuits delivered prescriptions by motorbike. Like many London buildings it's old on top & modern underneath. How does that work?

The drugstore is now a McDonald's

Peter Jones - John Lewis's architecturally radical flagship. It's still a co-operative enterprise, though the employees no longer live upstairs.

Sloane St.

Sloane Square

Royal Court Theatre

Sloane Square

"Chelsea Tractors"

The King's Road suddenly everyone has a pram or a small dog...

Royal Hospital Chelsea was founded by Charles II in 1689. "Ex-armed-services residents over the age of 65 are entitled to wear its scarlet uniform"

Lower Sloane Street

The National Army Museum

Charge!
The museum of London comes to life! If you are up early enough you might see the Royal Horse Guards sweep through the Kensington streets on their "watering order."
From an upper room, high in one of the crumbling wedding-cake mansions, an early-riser is playing Barry Manilow.
"At the Copa ~ Copa Cabana!"
The ride is a relic of the days when horsemen left the barracks in the early hours to collect the day's water.
The Watering Order
takes place at 7am each morning, serving as exercise for the horses and riders not taking part in the day's Queen's Life Guard. The ride takes one hour.

WALK THE WILD LIFE

Bayswater Road — Marble Arch

Park Lane

dogwalkers & runners

Speaker's Corner

cormorants

The Serpentine is a designated bird sanctuary

West Carriage Drive

Animals in War

By the Round Pond

surrounded by fairies, rabbits & squirrels, stands on an artificial rock.

Walk to the middle of

Hyde Park

to hear the birds.

The Serpentine

Horses carrying military supplies advance warily toward danger through the Park Lane traffic around the Animals in War Memorial

An artificial lake with natural contours created in 1730 by damming the River Westbourne. You can fish here if you have a permit.

Exhibition Road

The Serpentine Gallery

The Albert Memorial

Shows four animals, each representing a continent: a bull for Europe, an Asian Elephant, an African camel and an American Buffalo

European Bull — Asian Elephant

Rotten Row for horse-riding

Hyde Park Gate — Kensington Road — Knightsbridge

Royal Albert Hall

I have great affection for the brown and glassy-eyed creatures in the

Natural History Museum

Science Museum

Albertropolis

In the Victoria & Albert museum, Tipoo's mechanical tiger endlessly and musically devours a British soldier at the turn of a handle

V & A

The Cromwell Road

To South Kensington — To Knightsbridge

Notting Hill was originally planned around a 'race-course'. Horse-racing attracted few backers and in 1842 the land was to attract London's rich to the "suburb" declined in value during synonymous with Rachman and race riots. During the 1990s are once again home to some of London's richest

To **Portobello Road Market** where last decade's designer goods are resold for a fraction of the original price ~ but when an item is old enough to be "vintage" its price begins to climb again.

Walk 8 ~ Labyrinth

Start Here

Elgin Crescent

Elgin Crescent

Landsdowne Road

Ladbroke Grove

Arundel G

Ladbroke

Lansdowne Crescent

St John's Gdns.

Por- broke Grove

This Estate Agent faces another on the opposite corner. Never has an area of London been sold and resold so frequently & for such varied sums.

Sapling trees show how new is the area's prosperity.

What's going on?

Is it an accident?

I can see her!!

Why is the road closed off?

or the police?

NO! V*** B**** is shopping in Matches.

Around

security guards

Matches Designer Boutique

course in 1836, which explains the area's _circular_ street pattern. sold for residential development. The grand Victorian villas designed the 20th century and were split up into flats, eventually becoming the area's _raffish_ charm attracted new buyers and the streets

Who goes around comes around.

The museum of Brands at 2 Colville mews collects the _must-haves_ of yesteryear.

The Electric Cinema

Portobello

Lonsdale Road

Westbourne Grove

Road

Ledbury Road

Denbigh Road

Kensington Park

Chepstow Villas

ington Park

Portobello Road

Pembridge

Road

dbroke sq.

Notting Hill

Westbourne Grove Church

houses _ten apartments_ in its eaves and rents out _fashion vitrines_ in its basement, which helped pay for its recent restoration.

She's coming out!... she has bags!

on the BUSES

(because London is a **RED BUS**)

Tourism on the cheap. Forget the tour buses. Take a busman's holiday in your own city.

Travel at the front of the top deck where you can experience a thrill when the bus rounds a corner...

Route **15** runs from Paddington through central London, past the Law Courts and the Tower of London, then on to Whitechapel, Poplar and Blackwall.

15 Paddington Station
Paddington
Edgware Road

Route **3** starts in the heart of London passing Whitehall before crossing the river to Lambeth, Kennington, Brixton and Crystal Palace.

Oxford Street

3

To Kensington

Marble Arch
Bond Street
Oxford Circus
Tottenham Court Road
Regent Street
Soho

Hyde Park
The Serpentine

Mayfair

The Albert Memorial

Piccadilly Circus
Haymarket
Trafalgar Square

Knightsbridge
Hyde Park Corner
Royal Academy
The Ritz

9
The Royal College of Art
Royal Albert Hall
Harrods
Harvey Nichols
Green Park
Whitehall
Westminster

Routemaster "heritage" route **9** is one of the shortest bus journeys in London at 5 miles (9 km)

Downing Street

Sloane Street Walk

The King's Road
Sloane Square
Houses of Parliament

To Hammersmith
Battersea Bridge

The Thames

Palace of Westminster

19 my favourite route starts in chic Chelsea and passes through central London shopping and theatreland, then on through fashionable Islington to bohemian Hackney

"Routemaster" vs Bendy Buses

After a gradual phasing-out, the last remaining Routemaster buses were withdrawn in 2005

the classic London Bus...

Highbury & Islington

upper street

Angel

Sadlers Wells

The unpopular "bendy buses" that replaced many Routemasters will be phased out by 2015 and replaced with new buses based on the Route-master.

Rosebery Avenue

The classic red London buses still run on two "heritage" routes, the **9** and **15**

Theobald's Road

Gray's Inn

Holborn

Shaftesbury Avenue

Royal Courts of Justice

The best view from a bendy bus? Facing backwards from the elevated rear seats*

Aldwych

Strand

Temple

Saint Paul's Cathedral

Whitechapel AA Gallery

Aldgate East

Aldgate

The City

To Limehouse, Poplar & Blackwall

Waterloo Bridge

Fleet Street

Mansion House

Cannon Street

Monument

Tower Hill

Tower Gateway

cross

Blackfriars Bridge

Southwark Bridge

London Bridge

Tower of London

The Imperial War Museum

Lambeth Palace

Lambeth Road

Kennington Road

To Crystal Palace

(the Palace that isn't there)

The transparent hall built for the 1851 Great Exhibition was moved to South London in 1854 and burnt down in 1936. The area and its football team have kept the name.

Tower Bridge

I ♥ London!

"If you stand long enough at Piccadilly Circus you will meet someone you know" (so "they" say)

100 years ago, Piccadilly Circus was considered to lie at the heart of London, the _hub_ of the British Empire ~ and, by extension, the world! Its clubs and bars were once a rendez-vous for Empire builders : today it's the centre of... what? A traffic island lit by _L.E.D. signs_ advertising global brands, it's a meeting point for foreign tourists ~but for London ~ers?

Anteros

The statue many mistake for Eros, God of Love, is actually his brother _Anteros_, the God of Love Returned, associated with charitable friendship, constructed as a memorial to the philanthropist Earl of _Shaftesbury_ in 1893. Although Anteros carries _lead_ arrows, he is the world's first light _aluminium_ statue.

Tate to Tate

Tired of walking? Take the boat.
Follow the trail of **Power**
(political, economic & turbine)
from bank to bank of the
Thames

Cleo...

Hungerford Bridge

The London eye

Waterloo...

Westminster Bridge

Palace of Westminster

Start at **Tate Britain**, the original White Cube gallery (Henry Tate, founder and chief benefactor, made his fortune in sug- ar).

St Thomas's Hospital

The Florence Nightingale museum

Saint Thomas's Hospital

The Thames

Millbank

boat stops here

Lambeth Bridge

Lambeth Palace: the seat of power in Christian Medieval London.

To **Battersea Power Station**, another powerhouse awaiting restoration.
Plans have gon full circle from a theme park to a shoppin mall & bac to an (eco) power supplier...

Vauxhall Bridge

Somerset House and The Courtauld Gallery ~ Inns of court ~ City of London ~

To Saint Paul's Cathedral.

The Tate Boat

Blackfriars Bridge

The Millennium Bridge

Cross the "wo and feel the Power bank

bbly bridge" balance of sway from to bank...

Southwark Bridge

boat stops here

The Oxo Tower: originally another London power station, then a beef stock cold store; now another restaurant/ art gallery/ shopping centre...

Tate Modern

An ex-power station. Now a power-house of art. The British Council reports* the "creative industries" are the fastest growing in the United Kingdom.

The National Theatre a rare 100% new-build regularly voted the most loved or hated building in Britain

Stop for lunch at Borough Market at the top of Borough High Street: organic and artisanal gourmet food.

County Hall

Once the powerhouse of London's local government: now an aquarium...

Skateboarders have converted the concrete curves around the National Theatre into the perfect skate ramp

Building on the Past

Space is at a premium along the riverbanks and old buildings are reborn as new. For the moment the balance of political power has settled on the North bank while, on the South Bank, Industry has been replaced by Leisure.

*"Culture and Creativity"-British Council 2007

"Overcity and..."

In his 1902 investigation into life in the East End, writer **Jack London** christened this area **The Abyss**

designed by Victorian favourite, architect Augustus Pugin in 1872

Rollercoa...

The new Docklands Light Railway was built onto old railway viaduct...

walk to The Undercity

Tower Gateway

Royal Mint St

Paper fortunes I: The Royal Mint is no longer licensed to print money on this street, having moved to Llantrisant in Wales.

Dock Street

East Smithfield

Tower of London

Saint Katherine Docks 19th-century warehouses turned penthouses and a millionaires' marina with a "Dickens" pub. A pretty walk...

Thomas More St

Vaughan Way

100 bus

Pennington

The Hwy

What did... expect to fi... in... **Wapping** Jack London ... mean streets .... Instead...

Wapping Hi... more penthouses

Saint Katherine Penthouses

Saint Katherine Way

The Thames

Topsy Turvy

In the days of the Abyss, the top floors of dockside tenements contained the least desirable residences. Late 20th-century high-rise blocks designed to solve the problem merely replicated it. Now new-build or warehouse conversion apartments mean waterside high-rises are millionaires' penthouses. Down is the new UP...

The Lower Depths: An archaeological dig by Prescot Street church uncovered layers of London's past including Roman glass A 15th century shoes

the DOCKLANDS Light Railway

~opened in 1987 and has been a major factor in the regeneration of the area as well as a great opportunity to look right into the locals' windows...

The DLR's driverless trains speed to Canary Wharf. Take the driver's seat (or where it would have been) for the best views over the Abyss...

er!

the Undercity

cycle lane

→ **WAPPING**

one way

s t r e e t

Wilton's Music Hall (one of

the amusements of the (19) undercity, delicate "barley-sugar" columns and papier maché balconies are under threat **Paper fortunes II**

c a n d l e   s t r e e t

St George in the East

Like many of the ex-warehouse apartments Nicholas Hawksmoor's 18th century church has a modern interior. The original was destroyed in a 1941 bombing raid.

Paper fortunes III: In 1988

Rupert Murdoch moved the presses of News International to Wapping from Fleet Street leading to a massive printers' strike. Though production has since been moved out of London security remains strong around "Former Wapping"

The Hwy

wapping wood

Few 19th century warehouses were left intact after WW II. This building ~now apartments~ retains its overhead "catwalks"

e **block** behind the high-rises on the waterfront lie streets new low-rise social housing (Tower Hamlets remains one of London's most deprived boroughs)

W a p p i n g   L a n e

G a r n e t   s t r e e t

Wapping Rose Garden

Wapping old stairs

Town of Ramsgate pub

~wapping

N.B.
If you get tired point, jump the 100 bus tours Wapping High Street in both directions (route -----)
* stats: Government office for London.

Ta+ no anas?

Above-ground, Canary Wharf is _all business_. Everyday activities — shopping, eating and transport — are hidden _underground_. Explore four floors (plus "street" and "promenade" levels) of space in this space-age city to emerge...

...dock of banana importers, financial centre while the banana

...overtook the apple in 1998

Wharf's curves grey with yellow, a colour British nature

R STATION !!

Underground walkways link subterranean shopping malls no need to see the sky...

Cabot Square
West Cabot Mall
Canary Wharf DLR
1 Canada Square
Canada Place? mall beneath the park
Cabot Place Mall
Canary Wharf Jubilee Line
Jubilee Park
to Churchill Place Mall
Heron Quay
Grime Street
Bank Street
under the Park Jubilee Place Mall
Heron Quays
upper Bank St

Imaginary City: Canary Wharf's space-age style is popular with action & sci-fi film makers. James Bond & '28 Weeks Later' were filmed here

footbridge — West India Quay

Clifford Chance — a Law firm in Upper Bank street — has an in-house gym, multi-faith prayer room & hairdresser

...blinking in the sunlight from under Bank street to cross the silver bridge over gleaming West India Quay

sweat patches

All banana plants are sterile and are _artificially reproduced_ from cuttings of the Cavendish variety. Honduran scientists are attempting to breed a _new_ variety to ensure the fruit's survival.

A surprising number of babies with mothers (or corers?). Do they live here?

what are these?

Banana Skins

Canary Wharf looks like the _future_ but which future? In ten years will it look like what we thought the future would look like in 2011 And how does it look from **Poplar?**

Hero. Q"...'s on the South side of the water was rebuilt around the Grade I ...ished "banana wall" structure of the original dock.

The Grocer 1998

FIDO LIDO

Contrails cross the London summer skies reminding us of leaving...

Like most London lidos this one was built in the 1930s (opened 1932) in response to new fashions for exercise and foreign holidays. Like many London lidos, it was closed due to cheaper package holidays and 80's council funding cuts. Unlike Victoria Park Lido (destroyed to create a car park) it has re-opened thanks to local effort and enthusiasm.

Water-colour pictures. The Lido's art space.

No nonsense: at the restored Hackney Lido, swimming is business-like and laned. If you want to picnic, you'll have to take it in the Park.

Parks

Well Street Common

Annual Report of the Registrar General, 1839

Royal Gate East

Victoria drinking fountain - for the pre-bottled water age (now fenced off) financed by reformer Angela Burdett-Coutts

Crown gate east

Victoria Park had its own speakers' corner with a fiercely left-wing reputation. Sylvia Pankhurst was arrested here in 1914

Victoria Park Road

women with babies

men with other men.

deer (really)

sports ground

A Japanese-style pagoda stood on this island but became derelict by the 1950s

Three colts bridge

skew bridge

molesworth gate

Cadogan gate

shelter under old London Bridge arches

saint Mark's Gate

~ Regent's Canal ~

Hackney Marsh

the proposed olympic site has caused controversy amongst environmentalists as well as some of the hundreds of Sunday league football teams playing here each week

DON'T FORGET!

Hackney's street battles ~ I mean the non-violent street-naming wars between genteel royalist terraces (Tudor Close and King Edward's Road) and reforming streets, Burdett Road (after Angela Burdett-Coutts) and Thurtle Road (after birth control campaigner, Dorothy Thurtle)

takes over the street each Sunday. At the bottom of Goldsmith's Row cross the Hackney Road to finally find the country, just as the city likes it.

Good morning, gardeners! Lovely day! If it's raining, it's just an illusion!

Whatever you think of the retro-fabulous fashions, the 'cool' tattoos and the fashionable dogs, the market has cherry-picked its past, kitsched it up and used it to make the street

DOM!

Walk 13 up the Apples & (cool) Pears) coolers

The Dove free house: Hackney's coolest pub

Broadway once the road down which traders walked their livestock to Smithfield Market. After falling into decline in the late 20th century it has been revived and now holds a chic Farmers' Market every Saturday

Regent's Canal, no longer a thoroughfare for commercial barges, is now used to cool the thick electricity cables that run along its bed.

21-28

Broadway Market

Regent's

canalside walks

Canal

Tamworth

A **city farm** that comes with a café you can hire for events. The animals are frequently lent out to local film-makers.

Haggerston Park

Hackney City Farm

Goldsmith's Row

To Cambridge Heath Station →

Hackney Road

Buses 26, 48 to Liverpool St

Columbia Road

Hackney City Farm's **Mulberry Tree** visit in **September** to steal a juicy purple berry.

WALK A-UPPER STREET

an area of **super-gentrification**: going from poverty to luxury in a generation. Along Upper Street, high-street shops have been replaced by design emporia selling strictly non-essential items: corsages, novelty washing-up gloves, hand-felted scarves...

To Holloway once more genteel than neighbouring Islington (when Mr. Pooter lived there in "Diary of a Nobody"). Now more gritty...

A green oasis: Highbury Fields

Highbury Corner marks the border.

saint Paul's Road — To Hackney — le Creuset

The Estorick Collection of Modern Italian Art — sabatier

39a

Highbury

farrow & ball

George Orwell lived on one side

Canonbury Square

Evelyn Waugh on the other.

Canonbury Square is now planted with a miniature vineyard sponsored by Loire Valley wines

The Hope & Anchor
Launch pad for British punk bands of the 1970s — 207

Alessi

Hotblack Desiato

Flamboyantly-monikered estate agent after which sometime Islington resident, Douglas Adams named a minor character in "The Hitchhiker's Guide to the Galaxy" — 105

Get Stuffed Taxidermist's. Have your ex-pet immortalised as a design object

Lost in the reshuffle Restaurant Granita used to be here the spot where Tony Blair & Gordon Brown did a deal that changed the face of UK politics in the 1990s — 127

The Screen on the Green — 83 delightful 1920s cinema

Business Design Centre — 52

Most of the essentials of life (supermarkets, banks, cheaper clothing shops) are hidden behind Upper Street on the Liverpool Road.

Liverpool Rd

cross street

114
314
Little Angels Children's Theatre

Islington Green

DIY & decor merchant's shops supply design-conscious Upper Street with new colours...

4 SAM (Sausage & Mash) cafe, preserved for its chic 1950s decor.

Times change and sometimes disappear. In 2009, landmark the Angel Clock vanished causing consternation amongst residents before reappearing equally mysteriously

To Central London

Chapel Market

Angel

Islin t n-HOME
Islington's "super~gentrification" has been driven by property prices. Is it any wonder there are so many estate agents and design shops along Upper Street?
The King's Head Pub & Theatre, like the nearby Hen & Chickens and the Red Lion, combines old~style Islington pub culture with new Islington culture.
The spire of St. Mary's Church
THEATRE
THEATRE
Upper Street is thick with delivery vans
They're for restoration!
Another homewares shop!
but they have really good pans.
...and when her pot plants stop flowering, she just bins them...
old & new fashionably mismatched
What's she doing with the old sofa?
West Upper Street: design shops with the odd estate agent.
East Upper Street: estate agents with the odd design shop
Old Islington is remade, restored and renovated – by the finest artisans

Market, Islington

At night the abandoned skeletons of the market stalls rattle eerily. The street is deserted except for a mysterious r-c--d figure. The jellied eel café operates from behind blacked-out windows as though something sinister goes on there...

M Manze Eels 4 Pies

15, Pentonville Road

first Ring Road?

tonville Road or "The new d from Paddington to ngton" as it was known in 6 when it was built as don's first bypass.

1945 it formed part of rick Abercrombie's first ndon Ring Road.

chapel market

M. Manze Eel 4 Pie shop (1902) — 74

white Lion street

Monopoly Money → the creators of the London board game, Monopoly, are said to have met at The Angel pub (now a bank) to perfect their design. It's no accident that several ~now pricey~ Islington streets are featured in the board's cheaper sets...

1859 cupola: The Angel Pub

Angel · Upper Street · Saint John St

Sundays ~ what are they for?

The busy city surrounding the market is dead at week-ends but Sunday is Spitalfield Market's busiest day. When the market's famous glass roof was raised in 1883 Sundays were for downing tools and worshipping at nearby Christ Church. Now they're for shopping but a very different kind from the dash for weekly essentials. **We buy:**

1 handmade jewellery...

2 vintage ~ or imitation~ vintage ~ clothes

3 luxury foods: coffee, olives, chocolate

Enormous new canteens hold up the **glass roof**

THE RE

S.M.U.T. called the pre-development market a **"Brightfield site"** (a focus of special value to the local community). Now that it's bright with neon & glass reflecting the vintage & handmade does it still do the job? And is this 'homebaked~in-techno' mix what a city looks like now?

During the last decade of the 20th century S.M.U.T. (Spitalfields market under threat) fought what they called urban de (not "re-") generation." Despite their campaign the old market was enclosed in the belly of a glass and steel whale designed by **Norman Foster**, in a process oddly similar to Robert Horner's 19th century redevelopment. The market porter turned market owner destroyed historically valuable 17th century buildings but put in place the market that S.M.U.T. tried to preserve unchanged as opposed to "brownfield"~ or previously developed site for redevelopment

small vanities: during the market's renovation, a Roman cemetery was discovered. "Spitalfields Woman" a fashionable 20-something, was found well-preserved in her lead-lined coffin buried with silk & gold cloth

Friday Night on BRICK

DK17 the Cupcake Revolution

Two forces have transformed this area: **art and food**

"East End" entered the language around 1880* a little before "unemployment" (1882†) and sweatshop around 1892. These streets have seen "miles of bricks, squalor, and from each cross street and alley flashed long vistas of bricks and misery"

Brick Lane Beigel Bake: 24-hour bargain bagels which recall the street's 19th Century Jewish heritage. 159

Bethnal Green · Sclater Street

The Old Truman Brewery: Once Britain's largest staffed during the 17th & 18th centuries, by Huguenot (French Protestant) refugees. Now home to creative businesses, shops, bars, galleries and the Sunday "Up Market" 91

Brick Lane is lined with cheap and cheerful curry houses. Eat here or with the locals who are more likely to cross over to the Commercial Road.

Commercial · Brick Lane · Sunday Up Market

Lamb Street · Hanbury Street

Why CUPCAKES? they're **DIVERSE, Retro, Individualistic,** *Kitsch, artisanal & slightly too expensive*

Spitalfields market

Fournier Street

(appropriately) Fashion St

The Whitechapel Gallery Founded in 1901 at the height of Whitechapel's poverty with the radical aim of bringing art to the people: re-opened in 2009 after redevelopment doubling the gallery's size to include a respected restaurant

Osborn Street

Commercial Street is still all business. Unlike Brick Lane the City end is dead after 6pm

Aldgate East · Whitechapel · High St · Whitechapel · Docklands · Poplar · commercial road

Sunday Up Market

bricked-in windows

TRU... BLACK E...

*William Fishman: East End 1888

€ Oxford English Dictionary 1880

☆ The People of the Abyss: Jack London

Departures

There's more than one way to leave London. Tombstone~shaped _Necropolis_ railway station opened in 1854 to transport visitors and clients to _Brookwood_, one of a ring of **19th** century cemeteries built around London after city graveyards filled up. Until its destruction during a 1941 bombing raid, just as in life, coffined passengers travelled _first_ or _second_ class.

WESTMINSTER BRIDGE HOUSE

121

121

stone funeral drapery

On their way to somewhere else? wearing badges for a "Church of Jehovah conference."

'Boris' Bikes — named after the Mayor of London who intro~duced the scheme, these heavy~weight rental cycles are the latest way to leave Waterloo

Waterloo

The area around the station is~ perhaps surprisingly~ residential but, criss-crossed by railway bridges and sliced-through by roads, it has an oddly temporary feel...

As it's no longer possible to exit the city by the Necropolis Railway, return to Waterloo & take the Northern line to **Highgate**

THERE'S PROBABLY NO GOD NOW STOP WORRYING AND ENJOY YOUR LIFE

SPARO

William Blake, poet, artist & visionary lived, suspended between Heaven and Earth, on this site on **Hercules Road**

Now a blue~plaqued housing estate set, appropriately, opposite Eden caterers. Round the corner from Virgil Street lies Centaur Street where there is a magical railway tunnel lined with mosaics based on the artist's work as well as sound~boxes. Listen as local voices recite Blake's poetry at the touch of a button...

Waterloo station's necropolitan facade rises in dedication to the World War One dead who travelled from here...

York Road
Westminster Bridge Rd
Waterloo Rd
Bayliss Road
Kennington Road
Hercules Road
Virgil St

121
Necropolis mosaics here
Centaur St

St John's Waterloo
Lambeth North

The Imperial War Museum

The church's 18th century dead are stranded on a traffic island. In the crypt is the workshop for the Centaur Street Mosaics

Lambeth Rd

Highgate

The overgrown West Cemetery is appropriately home to the graves of many Pre-Raphaelite artists, painters of lush decay. Access to the West side is currently by daily guided tour only.

The most moving monuments look alive, not dead...

WALK 19 r.i.p.

⚠ DANGER UNSAFE KEEP AWAY

Living with the dead? Three spectacular glass cube modernist houses designed, like General Otway's vault, to be looked into from outside.

Terrace catacombs

Julius Beer's Mausoleum (look inside for the moving memorial to the News-paper proprietor's daughter.)

Radclyffe Hall

Faraday

Dissenters' cemetery

Egyptian Avenue

Dickens family vault

Elizabeth Siddal

The Lebanon circle: the cemetery's most famous landmark is built around 330-year-old cedar tree.

Christina Rossetti

Ford Madox-Brown

Entrance

General Otway, one of the first proud residents of the cemetery, had skylights set into the ground-level roof of his family vault

swain's Lane

The West Cemetery is romantically wild

but there's more to it than meets the eye. The 1839 cemetery buildings, made economically from rendered brick rather than stone, crumble picturesquely. The cemetery's wild appearance dates from the mid 20th century when it fell into disrepair. Maintained, since 1980, in a state of "managed neglect", several areas have been restored to a 19th-century neatness some visitors find shocking...

swain's Lane

City of the Dead

Perhaps the only "city" in London with no living inhabitants. Ironically these green and restful spaces (with such good company, too) are some of the best places in London to be alive...

Victorian pugilist, Thomas Sayers' kennel-shaped grave is guarded by his favourite dog

BORN AT PIMLICO BRIDGE

Highgate Village:
Olde-Worlde tea shops & nu~skool coffee bars...

Highgate Hill

Ten courts

Waterlow Park
"a garden for the gardenless" since 1889...

To Archway

Lauderdale House for food & arts events

Sidney Waterlow, benefactor

"A green thought in a green shade"? *
A plaque on a Highgate Hill wall marks the spot where poet Andrew Marvell's house was thought to have stood.
* Andrew Marvell: the Garden

The T.O.C. Karl Marx tea-room

George Eliot

Max Wall

Patri Caulfield

Sh Gi

The East Cemetery

Less picturesque than the West cemetery, you can still be buried here. As the cemetery is~ despite the presence of Karl Marx's grave~ a private enterprise, a grave can be had for between £10,000~£30,000

Chester Road

Stone dogs (lions, horses)? Angels? Lush plant and animal life? The city of the dead is **teeming with life!**

Walk 20 — The Spirits of Christmas

The "City of London" is of course not the whole city of London. Around 340,000 people work in the financial centre but only 8,000 live there. Between Christmas and New Year the population shrinks further as Londoners depart in search of a "traditional" Christmas leaving the City a ghost town...

"The city clocks had just gone three but it was quite dark already: it had not been light all day"*

Dickens' House, 48 Doughty Street

48

Farringdon

The Fox & Anchor
Serves porter in pewter pots   115

22   Chancery Lane   High Holborn   ← Gray's Inn Road

'Hol

'Hol

City PRECIN

Charterhouse street

Smith Field Market

Farringdon St.

The Citte of Yorke's "medieval" building and wood-panelled booths inside actually date from the 1920s....

Many London pubs are the ghosts of their former selves, resurrected apparitions of destroyed buildings recreated in the spirit of the originals.

Is a city its buildings, its history, its present population or its **Ghosts?**

Cock Lane

Where Samuel Johnson famously laid a ghost that turned out to be all **cock & bull**. Debunked in 176 the story is stil presented as a genuine haunting on popular London ghost tours

Is London the world's most haunted city?   New Fetter Lane   Fe Ifer Lane

Dr. Johnson's House Gough Sq

145

Aldwych

Fleet Street

Ye Olde Cock Tavern
One of Dickens' favourite pubs was restored after a fire in **1990**

The Black Friar's
"medieva panels are earl twentieth century

The Strand

The Edgar Wallace named after the prolific mystery writer   40

Milford Lane

"One night's drunkenness may defeat the labours of forty days well employed"

Ye Olde Cheshire Cheese
Both Dickens and Johnson drank in this 1667 building (restored after the **Great Fire of London**) Is the Cheshire Cheese the real thing?   174

Blackfriars

→ The → Victoria → Embankment → → →

The Thames

Waterloo Bridge

"He had no further intercourse with spirits but lived upon the total abstinence principle..."

* Charles Dickens: A Christmas Carol ☆ Samuel Johnson – Letter to Boswel

Smithfield, 5am N.Y.

The market starts at 4am. By the time the last ☆ of the old year is fading, the market traders are packing up to go home

dawn over East London

The Temple of Meat was built in the same Victorian neoclassical style as the era's museums and railway stations by Horace Jones in 1868...

The architect designed many market halls as well as a lunatic asylum

The market's pale ribs arch over its dark flesh...

cctv

Didn't the Smithfield pubs used to open at 6am so the workers could have breakfast & a pint?

Some still do - around 7am. But I've got to load this lot up and drive back to Hampshire

A "heritage" blood-red phone box

Starbucks is open...

hard hat (to guard against falling carcasses?)

sweepings from butchers' stalls, dung, guts and blood drowned puppies, stinking sprats all drenched in mud, dead cats and turnip tops come tumbling down the flood *

blood stains

* A City Shower ~ Jonathan Swift

...y..ar's Eve

The Goddesses of Smithfield are statues representing London, Dublin, Liverpool & Edinburgh

Smithfield's future is not secure despite a successful appeal against redevelopment proposals in 2008...

...during the next decade the market's lease will expire. With pressure from developers growing, could Smithfield become another Spitalfields?

Carcasses hang like East End gangsters in the movies...

white van

The Sunset Café-Bar has opened to serve weak coffee in polystyrene cups

Walk 21 — Meat

St John restaurant famous for "nose to tail eating"; nothing left except the squeal

The Eagle claims to be London's first gastropub (opened in 1991)

159 Farringdon

saint John street

Clerkenwell Green — ☐ hasn't been green for the last 300 years

Karl Marx Memorial Library

To clerkenwell Road

Farringdon

Fabric nightclub 77a

2

Charterhouse street

"gastropub" (noun): a term coined in the 1990s from the words "pub" + "gastronomy", describing a pub serving good food

Smithfield is surrounded on all sides by bars, restaurants & clubs: a different kind of Meat Market.

West Smithfield

Snow Hill Tunnel (closed 1916) now part of the London Underground

Snow Hill enabled the transport of animal carcasses to Smithfield by train.

Holborn Viaduct

Farringdon street

The Black Friar

174 Queen Victoria Street. The shape of a wedge of cheese, the pub was decorated in 1903 by Henry Poole & H. Fuller Clark with relief panels of jolly Friars. Look for the monk boiling an egg. This gastro-pub's speciality is pies

174

black-friars

in London for New Year

on water

Walk 22 Victoria Embankment · **Cleopatra's Kiosk**

The pretty gardens along the North banks of the Thames are a cover for Joseph Bazalgette's great Victorian sewer system.

Westminster Bridge · Westminster

Hungerford Bridge 3 to design the steel structure confectionary A · Embankment

When the humble original w destroyed to make way for 200 architects compete new glass and selling postcard I ♥ London

T-Shirts

"**Who** would pursue
The smoky glory of the town,
That may go till his native earth
And by the shining fire sit down
Of his own hearth,
Free from the griping scriveners' bands,
And the more biting mercers' books
Free from the bait of oiled hands
And painted looks? **»** *

✠ Samuel Johnson ✠ Misha Black's 'District' design ＊ Sir Richard Fanshawe, An Od

NO! YOUR OWN TRIP STARTS *here*

acknowledgements:

Thanks Alice, Roger, James, Beth: Thanks Hannah

The author would like to acknowledge gratefully
the support of the Authors' Foundation

First published 2011 by order of the Tate Trustees
by Tate Publishing, a division of Tate Enterprises Ltd,
Millbank, London, SW1P 4RG
www.tate.org.uk/publishing
Designed by Jason Godfrey
Printed and bound in China by C&C Offset Printing Co. Ltd.

A catalogue record for this book is available
from the British Library.
ISBN 978 1 85437 938 2